impact

4

Grammar Book

T0343858

NATIONAL GEOGRAPHIC
L E A R N I N G

Australia · Brazil · Mexico · Singapore · United Kingdom · United States

impact
4
Grammar Book

Embedded clauses, questions and commands

Adding emphasis

Free-climbing the Dawn Wall in Yosemite National Park, United States

Embedded clauses, questions and commands

> **Embedded clauses**, **questions** and **commands** are part of, or embedded in, a longer sentence. Generally, they are preceded by a clause.
>
> When embedding a statement, the word order remains the same.
> *Extreme sports are dangerous.* ———▶ *I think **extreme sports are dangerous**.*
>
> When embedding a question, the word order changes to that of a statement if the question becomes a statement.
> *What obstacles has Cory overcome?* ———▶ *I wonder **what obstacles Cory has overcome**.*
>
> When embedding a question that continues to be a question, the word order changes to that of a statement, because <u>a new clause</u> has taken over the question function.
> *Can we climb that mountain?* ———▶ <u>*Do you know*</u> ***if we can climb that mountain**?*
>
> When embedding a command, we use the infinitive with *to*.
> *Try downhill mountain biking.* ———▶ *I'm asking you **to try downhill mountain biking**.*

1 **Read the sentences.** Rewrite them using embedded clauses, questions and commands.

Example: *I am going to like mountain biking!*
      I think *I am going to like mountain biking!*

1. I want to try skiing.

   I think _____.

2. Can we go up the mountain?

   I wonder if _____.

3. They will enjoy going fast.

   They believe _____.

4. Try it once, at least.

   I'm asking you _____.

5. I won't be any good at it.

   I know _____.

6. How difficult is it?

   Do you know _____?

2 **Choose *to, if* or – (no change).**

Example: *I told you **to** try mountain biking!*

1. I wonder _____ it is worth doing.

2. I think _____ it looks scary but a lot of fun!

3. My dad told me _____ have a go.

4. She doesn't know _____ I will like it.

5. I believe _____ I will overcome my fear.

6. I told myself _____ go for it!

3 **Match the sentence beginnings with the embedded clauses.** Write sentences. Make any necessary changes.

1. Do you know   a. Can I learn to surf here?

2. He's wondering   b. She will go to the beach today.

3. I think   c. I am going to be good at this.

4. I'm telling you   d. They provide boards at the surf shop.

5. She has decided   e. Try body boarding!

6. I wonder   f. He is able to surf.

1. _Do you know if they provide boards at the surf shop?_

2. _____

3. _____

4. _____

5. _____

6. _____

4 **Use the prompts to write sentences with embedded clauses, questions or commands.**

Example: *think / new sport / difficult*

I think trying a new sport is difficult.

1. wonder / snowboarding / weekend

_____

2. know / slope / open

_____

3. ask / try / tobogganing

_____

4. guess / prefer / summer

_____

5. remember / play / beach

_____

6. not know / climb / mountain

_____

Adding emphasis

We can add a clause at the beginning of a sentence to add emphasis. This focuses attention on the original statement.

We use a noun (*the thing, the place, the day, the time, the reason,* etc.) to say where, when, why or who, or use the word *what* at the beginning of the sentence.
The reason (why) *I won't go surfing is that I don't like swimming in the sea.*
The place (where) *my sister loves hiking is the Himalayas.*
The thing (that) *he loves about yoga is that it makes him feel relaxed.*
What I really like is *swimming in rivers.*

REMEMBER

Note that *wh-* words other than *what* do not generally work with these statements. We use a noun instead.
Where *my sister loves hiking is the Himalayas.* ✘
The place (where) *my sister loves hiking is the Himalayas.* ✔

When the clause begins with a noun, the *wh-* word (or *that*) can be omitted.
The reason (why) *I won't go surfing is that I don't like swimming in the sea.*
The thing (that) *he loves about yoga is that it makes him feel relaxed.*

1 **Match the two halves to make complete sentences.**

1. The place
2. The reason
3. The time
4. The moment
5. The feeling
6. The mood

a. I have when I'm surfing is that it's good to be alive!
b. I prefer to surf is in the early morning, when it is less crowded.
c. I love the most is the beach.
d. I'm in after surfing is always positive.
e. I go to the beach is to surf.
f. I love the most is watching the sunrise.

2 **Put the words in order.** Write the sentences.

Example: *reason / Dad / the / is / why / won't / heights / his / climbing / of / fear / go*
   The reason why Dad won't go climbing is his fear of heights.

1. the / most / like / I / climbing / rock / sport / is

_____

2. I / reason / climbing / for / is / the / physical / started / a / workout

_____

3. most / I / like / having / to / concentrate / the / thing / is

_____

4. hill / a / behind / is / place / my / town / like / best / I / the

_____

5. started / new / a / sport / that / try / to / climbing / I / the / reason / is / wanted / I

_____

6. Saturday / the / day / climbing / is / for / I / set / aside

_____

3 **Read the sentences.** Rewrite them adding emphasis. Use your own ideas.

Example: *I don't like contact sports because I am small.*
   The reason *I don't like contact sports is because I am small.*

1. I love running because it makes me feel relaxed.

_____

2. I don't like swimming in the sea. There is too much seaweed.

_____

3. I prefer cycling in summer.

_____

4. I love playing netball with my friends.

_____

5. I enjoy running in the park the most.

_____

6. I love going for a run in the early morning.

_____

WRITING

Write five opinions and justifications for liking or disliking an activity. Use embedded clauses for the opinions and add emphasis to the justifications.

Example: ***I think*** *rugby is a dangerous sport.* ***The reason*** *I think this is because there are many injuries every game.*

Future tenses

Quantifiers

Men working together to move a roof, Bangladesh

Future tenses: Describing events in the future

We use the **future simple** (*will* + bare infinitive):
- to make predictions.

Over the next few years, people **will look** *online to find volunteers to help with disaster relief.*
- communicating spontaneous decisions.

I'll go *to the shops in a minute.*
- to talk about future facts.

The global population **will continue** *to grow in the 21ˢᵗ century.*
- to make promises.

We **will help** *you to rebuild your house after the earthquake.*
- for questions and requests.

Will *you* **raise** *funds for the reconstruction effort?*
- for suggestions. Only *I* or *we* is used for suggestions, however.

Shall I *come with you?*

We use the **future continuous** (*will* + *be* + *-ing*):
- to talk about the duration of a future action.

I'll be working *in Mexico for a year.*
- for an action that is in progress at a specific time in the future.

What **will you be doing** *at 8 o'clock tomorrow?*

We use the **future perfect** (*will* + *have* + past participle) for an action that will be complete by a specific time in the future, or before another future action.

By the time I am 50, scientists **will have discovered** *many new ways to help humanity.*

➔ See irregular verbs list on page 52.

1 **Complete the sentences with the verbs in the box.** Use the future continuous.

raise	volunteer	~~work~~	run	donate	hold

Example: *I* ***will be working*** *on the beach clean-up this time next week.*

1. They _____ a fundraiser this evening.

2. My best friend _____ at an animal shelter every Thursday this year.

3. My sister _____ a half-marathon for an animal charity next weekend.

4. She _____ funds at work all week.

5. We _____ the money from our cake sale to the charity.

2 **Rewrite the statements as questions.** Then write a negative answer.

Example: *He will be helping us this afternoon.*
Will he be helping us this afternoon? *No,* **he won't be helping us this afternoon.**

1. They will be volunteering to clean up the park next week.
   _____ No, _____.

2. You will be organising a cake sale.
   _____ No, _____.

3. My friend will be helping out at a local library.
   _____ No, _____.

4. The group will be holding a fundraiser this evening.
   _____ No, _____.

5. We will be giving up our time at the weekend to help the charity.
   _____ No, _____.

3 **Circle the correct answer.**

Example: *What _____ at 7 p.m.?*   a. *will you do*   b. *are you do*   c. *will you be doing*

1. _____ me with the beach clean-up?   a. Will you be helping   b. Are you help   c. Will help

2. Tomorrow morning they _____ to a talk on plastic pollution.   a. will listening   b. listening   c. will be listening

3. I believe he _____ in raising the necessary funds.   a. will be succeeding   b. will succeed   c. succeeding

4. The coordinator _____ out sponsorship forms today.   a. will be handing   b. will handing   c. hands

5. Our project _____ tomorrow morning.   a. launch   b. will launching   c. will be launching

6. The charity _____ a fundraiser next weekend.   a. will be holding   b. will holding   c. it will hold

4 **Complete the sentences with the future perfect.** Use the verbs in the box.

be	make	spend	~~start~~	stop	take

Example: *We* **will have started** *the beach clean-up by the time you arrive.*

1. Everyone _____ for a break at around 11 a.m., so you can join us.

2. The volunteers _____ the rubbish away in bags.

3. We _____ in Canada for six weeks by then.

4. By the end of the week, we _____ about €600.

5. The campaign _____ a big difference to the coastal environment in this area.

When we talk about quantities, we need to know whether to use a singular or a plural verb.

We use a singular verb with singular nouns, or fractions/portions of singular nouns.

Half of/Fifty per cent of *the world's population* **is** ...

The majority of/Most of *the population* **is** ...

The number of *radio stations worldwide* **is** *51,000.*

We use a plural verb with plural nouns, or fractions/portions of plural nouns.

The majority of/Most *people* **are** ...

A number of *radio stations* **are** *online.*

A lot of/Two-thirds of/Sixty-seven per cent of *the people* **are** ...

1 (Circle) the correct option.

Example: *A lot of young people* **is** /(**are**) *online for more than two hours a day.*

1. Half of some countries' population **is** / **are** under 18.

2. Over half of the people in some British towns **is** / **are** over 65.

3. The majority of my friends **has** / **have** a smartphone.

4. The majority of Africans **is** / **are** under 30.

5. Forty per cent of North America's population **is** / **are** under 30.

6. There **is** / **are** 51,000 radio stations worldwide.

7. An older person **is** / **are** less likely to listen to the radio online than young people.

8. Over half of the world **is** / **are** under 30.

2 **Match the two halves to make complete sentences.**

1. Most children in the UK	a. is nine.
2. Sixty per cent of Americans	b. start school at the age of five.
3. The number of French Nobel prize winners	c. donate money to charity.
4. Almost half of the American population	d. is more than ten tonnes.
5. The majority of the world's umbrellas	e. is obese.
6. The amount of rubbish collected	f. are produced in Songxia, China.

3 **Use the prompts to write sentences.** Use a singular or plural verb.

Example: *less than half / population / every day*
> ***Less than half of the world's population watches television every day.***

1. a lot / older people / Internet

   _____

2. more than two billion / Asians / online

   _____

3. 52 per cent / South America / under 30

   _____

4. 25 per cent / people in computing jobs / women

   _____

5. 24 per cent / teenagers / online 'constantly'

   _____

6. the number / American teenagers online / about 94 per cent

   _____

4 **Write six sentences about people in your class.**

Example: ***The majority of people in my class are girls.***

1. _____
2. _____
3. _____
4. _____
5. _____
6. _____

WRITING

Write four sentences making predictions about the future, using future tenses and quantifiers. Use the ideas in the box to help you.

Example: *By 2050,* ***most people will have switched*** *to electric vehicles.*

wearable technology	life on other planets	animals becoming extinct
population increases	extreme weather	advances in medicine

Mixed conditionals
Double comparatives

An Alaskan woman kissing a sockeye salmon that she caught

Mixed conditionals: Expressing how things would be different

Type 2 conditional sentences describe unlikely but possible scenarios. Both sentences refer to the present.

If + past simple + *would/could/might* + verb (bare infinitive)

If I **were** a better cook, I **would enjoy** my food more.

He **would be** a better cook **if** he **paid** attention to the recipes.

Type 3 conditional sentences describe scenarios which can't be changed. Both sentences refer to the past.

If + past perfect + *would/could/might* + *have* + past participle

If I **had learnt** some new recipes, I **would have enjoyed** cooking more.

We can use **mixed conditional sentences** to describe how situations would be different. In these sentences, the *if* clause and the main clause do not have to refer to the same time period.

To form a mixed conditional sentence to talk about an imagined past event with a present result use:

If + past perfect + *would/could/might* + bare infinitive or *be* + *-ing*.

If you **had learnt** to cook, you **wouldn't eat** pizza all the time.

If I **hadn't learnt** about overfishing, I **would** still **be eating** tuna.

➲ See irregular verbs list on page 52.

1 **Match the two halves to make mixed conditional sentences.**

1. If you hadn't lived in Hong Kong,
2. If I hadn't chosen the fish,
3. Europeans would not have coffee
4. If we hadn't used so much chilli,
5. If the oceans hadn't been overfished,
6. If you hadn't written down the recipe,

a. I wouldn't be feeling ill now.
b. we would not be worried about eating tuna.
c. you wouldn't know how to use chopsticks.
d. I wouldn't know how to make the dish.
e. if Columbus had not discovered America.
f. we would be able to eat the curry!

2 **Complete the Type 2 conditional sentences.** Use the ideas in the box.

> visit Thailand   be a much better cook   eat insects   start to feel unwell
> ~~cook more interesting dishes~~   discover new flavours and ingredients

Example: *If I had more time, **I would cook more interesting dishes.***

1. If we didn't invest more money in food research, _____.
2. If I read more food books, _____.
3. If you ate spicy food every day, _____.
4. If I were old enough to travel, _____.
5. If I visited China, _____.

3 **Complete the Type 3 conditional sentences.** Use your own ideas.

Example: *If there had been a catering college in my town,* ***I would have become a chef.***

1. If I had lived in Columbus's era, _____.

2. If we had grown our own food, _____.

3. I would not have enjoyed it _____.

4. He would have eaten less healthy food _____.

5. If I had had more money, _____.

6. They would not have invented pasta _____.

7. We could have saved a lot of money _____.

8. If they had tasted the dish sooner, _____.

4 **Read the sentences.** Write a mixed conditional sentence.

Example: *I didn't save enough money. I can't go on holiday.*
  If I had saved enough money, I could go on holiday.

1. I didn't pass my exam. I'm not a chef.

_____

2. They went to China. They speak Chinese now.

_____

3. I bought a cheap oven. The food isn't cooked.

_____

4. You didn't wash your hands. I won't eat your cooking.

_____

5. I bought new glasses. I can read the recipe.

_____

6. He ate lots of biscuits. He feels sick now.

_____

7. We learnt how to bake. We have our own cake shop.

_____

8. I didn't learn about food hygiene. I have food poisoning.

_____

Double comparatives: Describing outcomes

In double comparative structures, the first part of the comparison expresses a condition and the second part expresses an outcome or result.

The more people there are in the world, **the more** food we need to produce.
The less our food travels, **the less** it impacts the environment.
The more we choose wholesome foods, **the healthier** we are.
The less we eat processed foods, **the better**.

REMEMBER

Fewer should only be used with countable nouns, while **less** should be used with uncountable nouns. For example, you can have **fewer** ingredients, vegetables, etc. but **less** salt, food, etc.

1 Complete the sentences with *fewer* or *less*.

Example: *The more he studies, the **less** stressed he feels.*

1. The more dangerous it is, the _____ people will try it.

2. The more time we spend here, the _____ time we'll have at the park.

3. The higher you climb, the _____ air there is in the atmosphere.

4. The older I get, the _____ friends I make.

5. The more tea I drink, the _____ coffee I drink.

6. The _____ mistakes you make, the better your mark will be.

2 Match the two halves to make complete sentences.

1. The more we know about food,	a. the fewer 'food miles' we create.
2. The less processed food we eat,	b. the more dehydrated you will become.
3. The more often we eat local food,	c. the better we can eat.
4. The less we overfish the seas,	d. the less money we spend at the supermarket.
5. The less water you drink,	e. the healthier we will be.
6. The more food we throw away,	f. the less we throw away.
7. The more vegetables we grow at home,	g. the more likely you are to like it.
8. The more we buy ugly vegetables,	h. the more food we need to eat.
9. The more exercise we do,	i. the more money we waste.
10. The more you try a certain food,	j. the less marine life we destroy.

3 **Complete the sentences with comparative phrases.** Use your own ideas.

Example: *The more we find out about food production,* **the more informed our choices can be.**

1. The more sugar we eat, _____.

2. The less we know about where our food comes from, _____.

3. The more restaurants you visit, _____.

4. The fewer resources we consume, _____.

5. The less time we have, _____.

6. The larger the farms we build, _____.

7. The further we are from where our food is grown, _____.

8. The more we grow locally, _____.

4 **Write your own sentences about how you can waste less food personally.** Use *the more/ less/fewer ... the ...*

Example: **The more I plan my meals, the less food I have to buy.**

1. _____

2. _____

3. _____

4. _____

5. _____

6. _____

WRITING

Write five conditional sentences and sentences with double comparative structures so that they have similar meanings.

Example: ***If I knew*** *more about food production,* ***I would*** *choose my food more carefully.*

 The more *I find out about food production,* ***the more*** *carefully I choose my food.*

Passives

Verbs followed by gerunds or infinitives

Japanese fans wave rubbish bags before cleaning up after a World Cup game.

Passives: Describing actions and processes

We use the **passive voice**:
- to emphasise the action rather than the person who did it (the agent).

Plastic bottles ***are polluting*** *the planet.*
- when we don't know who is doing the action.

Billions of plastic bottles ***are produced*** *every year.*
- when it is easy to understand who is doing the action.

The issue ***is highlighted*** *in Jack Johnson's music.*

The passive voice is formed with *be* + past participle.

What ***has been done*** *...?*

Sustainability ***is being promoted*** *...*

The ideas ***will be passed*** *on ...*

The negative is formed by putting the word *not* after the auxiliary verb.

The majority of plastic bottles ***are not recycled*** *at all.*

➡ See irregular verbs list on page 52.

1 **Rewrite the active sentences as passive sentences.**

Example: *People have bought too many plastic bottles. (buy)*
  Too many plastic bottles have been bought.

1. They don't sell plastic bottles at Jack Johnson concerts. (sell)

   _____

2. This will encourage fans to bring reusable water bottles to the concerts. (encourage)

   _____

3. Manufacturers produce billions of bottles a year. (produce)

   _____

4. We have used too much plastic. (use)

   _____

5. We don't recycle most of our plastic water bottles. (recycle)

   _____

6. Plastic waste is harming animals. (harm)

   _____

2 Complete the sentences with *is, isn't, should, shouldn't, will* or *won't*.

Example: *A lot of plastic **isn't** manufactured in the country where it is sold.* ✗

1. Most bottles you use once _____ be recycled. ✗

2. Instead, they _____ be thrown into landfill. ✔

3. Many _____ be diverted to the ocean. ✔

4. Plastic _____ found in the marine food chain. ✔

5. It _____ digested by marine animals. ✗

6. Food _____ gradually replaced by plastic in the stomachs of seabirds. ✔

7. If we have to use it, all plastic _____ be separated and recycled. ✔

8. It _____ just be thrown away in the hope that it won't harm the environment. ✗

3 Rewrite the sentences with a passive verb.

Example: *People have used plastic for many purposes over the last 30 years.*
  Plastic has been used for many purposes over the last 30 years.

1. Plastic has replaced paper bags and cardboard trays.

   _____

2. Manufacturers could produce plastic more cheaply.

   _____

3. Marine animals ingest plastic.

   _____

4. People aren't recycling and reusing plastic enough.

   _____

5. Plastic is polluting our oceans.

   _____

6. It has harmed hundreds of species of marine wildlife.

   _____

7. A global effort will reduce the harm caused by plastic.

   _____

8. People shouldn't throw away plastic products.

   _____

> **WRITING**
>
> Write your top five rules for reducing plastic. Write your sentences in the passive.
>
> Example: *Your own bags **should be used** when shopping.*

Verbs followed by gerunds or infinitives

Certain verbs are followed by **infinitives**.

*Most water parks **want to use** less water.*

*Park employees **encourage** visitors **to keep** water inside the pool.*

Other verbs are followed by **gerunds**.

*How can they **avoid wasting** water?*

Some verbs can be followed by either, but sometimes with a difference in meaning.

*He **remembered to go** to the park.*

*He **remembered going** to the park.*

➲ Use the list on page 152 of the Student's Book to learn them.

1 **Complete the sentences with the gerund.** Use the verbs in the box.

| collect | go | have | recycle | say | separate | ~~take~~ | tell | wash |

Example: *I don't mind **taking** the rubbish to the recycling centre.*

1. Has your town started _____ plastic yet?

2. My brother keeps _____ me to save water.

3. I'm not that keen on _____ to the landfill site.

4. Do you think it's worth _____ your rubbish into different piles for recycling?

5. I regret not _____ my own bags at the shop. I had to pay to buy plastic ones.

6. Why does he object to _____ the car?

7. Forgive me for _____ this, but you need to recycle more.

8. My cousin's interested in _____ rainwater in a container in the garden.

2 **Match the questions to the answers.**

1. Do you like to use rainwater in the garden?

2. What else do you suggest for saving water?

3. How do you prevent your lawn drying up?

4. Would you like to have a swimming pool?

5. Do you have any other tips for green gardeners?

6. Now that you live in a flat, do you miss having a garden?

a. I suggest planting less thirsty plants in the garden.

b. Yes. I would encourage them to grow bee-friendly flowers.

c. Yes. I collect it from the roof in a large tank.

d. A bit, I suppose. But I enjoy spending time in the nearby public gardens.

e. I would hate to have one! They waste so much water! I can swim in the river!

f. I haven't got a lawn, but you could try planting shrubs around the lawn to give more shade.

3 **Complete the sentences about water conservation using an infinitive or a gerund rather than a noun.** Use your own ideas.

Example: *I think we should try **to develop ways of conserving water.***

1. I would like _____.

2. When I think about solutions to water shortages, I imagine _____.

3. We enjoy _____.

4. We should encourage people _____.

5. My parents admit _____.

6. You should consider _____.

4 **Look at the pairs of sentences.** Tick the correct sentence. (Sometimes, both sentences might be correct.)

Example: *a. I remember being told to recycle the newspapers.* ✔

b. I remember being told recycling the newspapers. ✘

1. a. My pet didn't like to be seen by the vet. ☐

b. My pet didn't like being seen by the vet. ☐

2. a. I was asked to take shorter showers. ☐

b. I was asked taking shorter showers. ☐

3. a. The director enjoyed to be filmed. ☐

b. The director enjoyed being filmed. ☐

4. a. Dad hates being interrupted. ☐

b. Dad hates to be interrupted. ☐

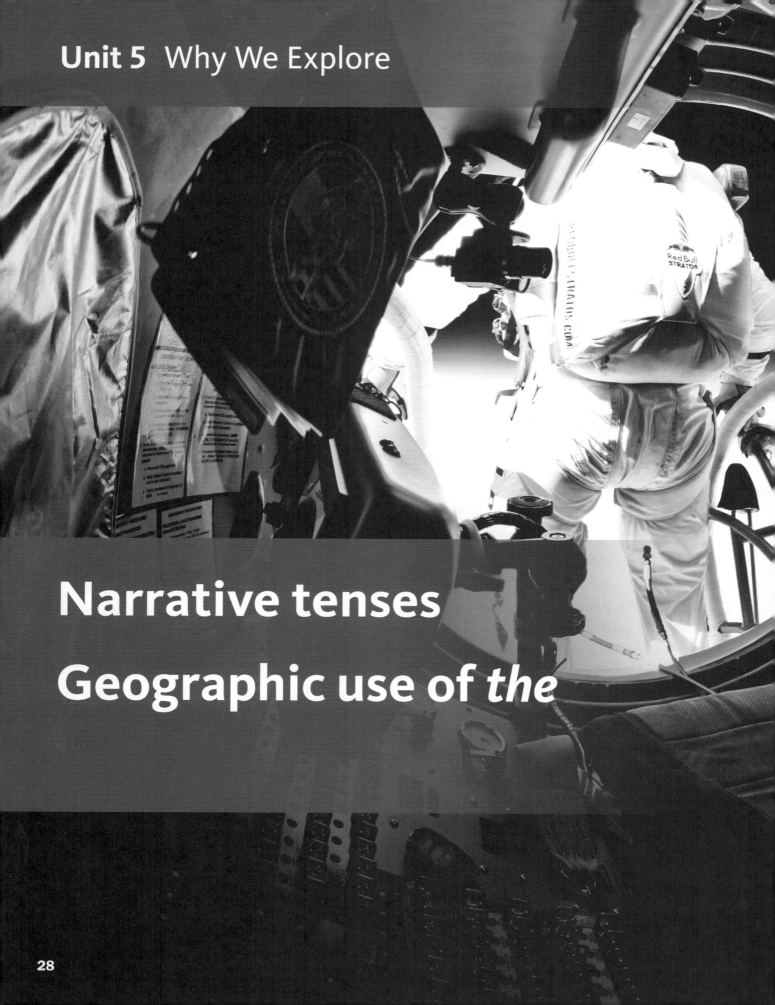

Narrative tenses

Geographic use of *the*

Austrian BASE jumper Felix Baumgartner jumps from the edge of space, 39 km. (24 mi.) above the surface of the Earth.

Narrative tenses: Telling a story

When we tell a story set in the past, we can use four different tenses:
- the **past simple** for completed actions in the past and for narrating past events in chronological order.
*He **closed** the cockpit, **switched on** his engine, **checked** his instruments and **taxied** towards the runway.*
- the **past perfect** to refer to an action completed in the past before another action in the past.
*He found a manufacturer to build an aeroplane from donated parts that **he had received**.*
- the **past continuous** to talk about actions that were in progress at a particular time in the past.
*The sun **was shining** and the birds **were singing** as he walked over to his plane.*
- the **past perfect continuous** to show that one action had finished before another in the past.
*He **had been waiting** on the runway for 10 minutes before he was cleared to take off.*

1 **Complete the table.** Use the Irregular verbs list on page 52 if necessary.

Verb	Present participle	Past participle
prepare	preparing	prepared
receive		
feel		
fly		
be		
learn		
offer		
accept		
go		
start		
meet		

2 **Change the sentences from the past simple to the past perfect.**

Example: *The adventurer crossed the Atlantic in record time.*
*The adventurer **had crossed** the Atlantic in record time.*

1. She made an emergency landing in the Egyptian desert.

   _____

2. She flew non-stop across the whole continent.

   _____

3. I found out a lot about her journey online.

   _____

4. My friend and I read the blog.

   _____

5. We were fascinated by her exploits.

   _____

3 **Change the sentences from the past simple continuous to the past perfect continuous.**

Example: *He was learning to fly for years.*
*He **had been learning** to fly for years.*

1. I was climbing the mountain.

   _____

2. We were standing on the summit.

   _____

3. My friends were coming up to join us.

   _____

4. I was hiding behind a rock.

   _____

5. We were celebrating our ascent.

   _____

4 **Use your answers from Activity 3.** Add another clause in a different tense.

Example: *He had been learning to fly for years **when he flew his first jet.***

1. _____
2. _____
3. _____
4. _____
5. _____

Geographic use of *the*

We use *the* with names of:
- mountain ranges.

Edmund Hillary went climbing in **the Himalayas**.
- rivers/oceans/seas.

John Hanning Speke discovered the source of **the Nile**.
- groups of islands.

Columbus discovered **The Bahamas**.
- points on the globe.

Amundsen's expedition was the first to reach **the South Pole.**
- general areas.

Alabama and Mississippi are considered part of **the South**.
- some countries.

Lewis and Clark crossed **the United States**.

We capitalise *the* when it forms part of a name.

I live in **The** *Hague in the* (not part of the name) *Netherlands*.

We don't use *the* with most countries, cities, streets, mountains, continents or islands, but there are exceptions to this!

1 Tick if *the* is needed in the sentence.

Example: *In around 1427, The Azores were discovered.* ✔

1. It is possible that **the** Antarctic peninsula was first seen in 1820. ☐
2. Gertrude Bell was an early European explorer of **the** Middle East. ☐
3. **The** Mont Blanc is the tallest peak in the Alps. ☐
4. A Frenchwoman explored **the** South Pacific in the 1700s disguised as a man. ☐
5. The longest lake in the world is **the** Lake Tanganyika. ☐
6. **The** Mount Kilimanjaro was first climbed in 1889. ☐

2 Complete the sentences with *the* or – (if *the* isn't needed).

Example: *Last year, we went on holiday to* **the** *Philippines.*

1. _____ Cuba is the largest Caribbean island.

2. Amundsen was the first person to reach _____ South Pole.

3. _____ South Africa is wild in parts, with large game species roaming free.

4. The explorer travelled to _____ West Indies.

5. _____ Amazon rainforest is largely unexplored.

6. They journeyed through _____ India, and ended up in _____ Mumbai in _____ west.

3 Rewrite the sentences using capital or lower case letters where necessary.

Example: *Many English villages have a street named the street in them. It is usually the main street,*
and would once have been the only Street.
Many English villages have a street named **T**he **S**treet *in them. It is usually the main street,*
and would once have been the only **s**treet.

1. Many early explorers named places after geographical features, for example the rio grande, or 'large river'.

   _____

2. Gradually, European explorers began to name places after the sponsors of their expeditions, or their own rulers, for example lake Victoria in east Africa.

   _____

3. Andorra is a small european Country located between france and spain.

   _____

4. At almost 7,000 m., mount Aconcagua is the highest mountain in south america.

   _____

5. Kenya, the country, was named after mount kenya, the second highest peak in Africa after Kilimanjaro.

   _____

WRITING

Write a paragraph about explorers and the places they explored. Use as many of the four tenses covered in this unit as possible.

Example: *America is named after Amerigo Vespucci, who first established that Columbus* **had discovered**
a new continent. It was while **he was travelling** *along the east coast of South America that he*
made *this discovery. He* **had been trying** *to find east India.*

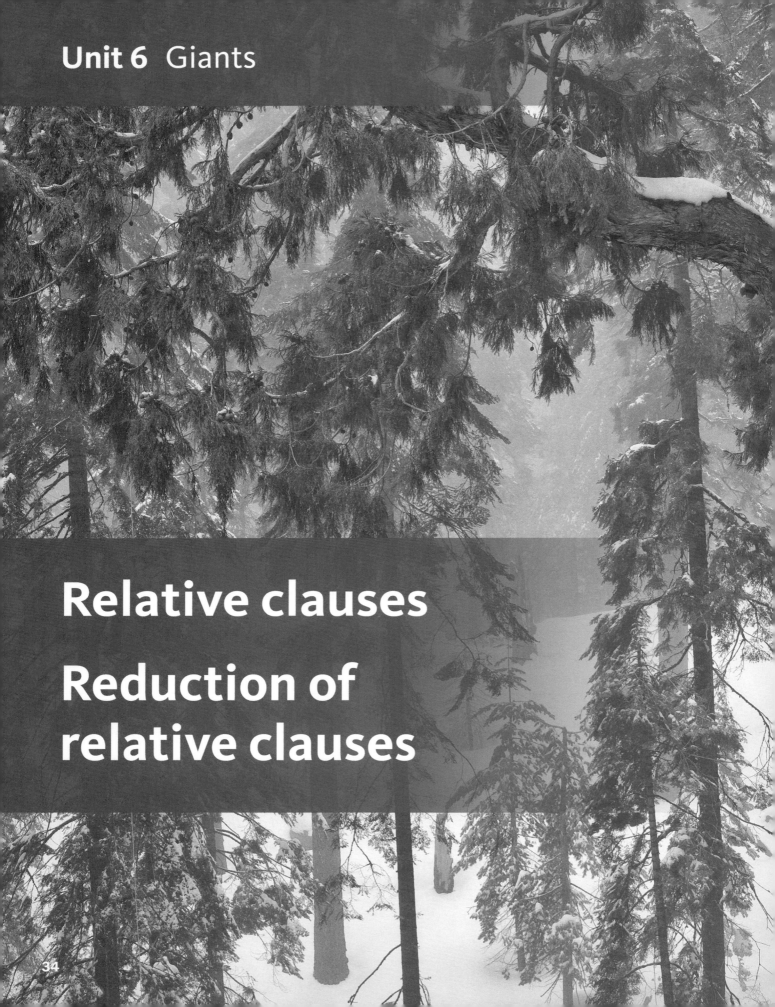

Relative clauses

Reduction of relative clauses

A team of scientists measuring a giant sequoia
in Sequoia National Park, California, USA

Relative clauses: Defining and describing

We use relative clauses to add an extra level of detail to a description in a sentence. We use *who* or *that* for people, *where* with places and *that* or *which* with things. We use *whose* to show possession. There are two types of relative clauses: defining and describing.

Defining relative clauses give defining information about the person, place or thing. If the clause is removed, the sentence loses its meaning.
*The ocean **where** megalodon swam was much warmer than the ocean is today.*

Describing relative clauses give extra descriptive information about the person, place or thing. This clause is placed between commas. If the clause is removed, the sentence still makes sense.
*Megalodon, **whose** name comes from the Greek giant tooth, had enormous jaws.*

1 **Circle** the correct option.

Example: *The ocean **where** / **that** megalodon swam was warmer than today's oceans.*

1. Scientists **which** / **who** study dinosaurs are called palaeontologists.

2. Dinosaurs **which** / **who** could fly were known collectively as pterosaurs.

3. Palaeontologists have discovered a species of giant dinosaur **which** / **who** had feathers.

4. The places **that** / **where** contain the most dinosaur fossils are deserts.

5. The blue whale, **which** / **who** is found in all the world's oceans, is larger than any dinosaur.

6. Marine biologists, **whose** / **that** job is to study life in the oceans, estimate that there are fewer than 25,000 blue whales left.

7. Giant sequoias, **that** / **which** are evergreens, are the world's largest trees.

8. A sperm whale, **which** / **that** is the largest animal with teeth, can dive to colossal depths to hunt.

2 **Use a defining relative clause to link the sentences together.**

Example: *I learnt about sharks in a documentary. It was very interesting.*
　　　　*I learnt about sharks in a documentary **that/which** was very interesting.*

1. It featured a woman in South Africa. She enjoyed swimming with great white sharks.

_____

2. She swam with the sharks. They mostly ignored her.

_____

3. My favourite dinosaur is the T. rex. It had a very small brain!

_____

4. It had a heart the size of a fridge. This was needed to pump blood through its 12-metre-long body!

_____

3 Use a describing relative clause to link the sentences together.

Example: *The woman I met was very interesting. She is an expert on giant trees.*

*The woman I met, **who is an expert on giant trees**, was very interesting.*

OR

*The woman I met, **who was very interesting**, is an expert on giant trees.*

1. Argentinosaurus is the largest dinosaur discovered so far. It was a herbivore.

   _____

2. The great white shark is the largest predatory fish. It is smaller than the whale shark.

   _____

3. The saltwater crocodile is the largest member of the crocodile family. It can grow to nearly six metres.

   _____

4. The largest bird on Earth is the ostrich. It is also the tallest.

   _____

4 Match the clauses to make complete sentences.

1. A baobab,

2. A blue whale's heart,

3. *Hyperion*,

4. The African forest elephant,

5. A male white rhino,

a. which is the name of a redwood in California,

b. which can weigh over two tons,

c. which is one of the largest trees in Africa,

d. which is smaller than the savannah elephant,

e. which is about the size of a quad bike,

i. is the world's tallest tree.

ii. beats at 8–10 beats per minute.

iii. is also in sharper decline.

iv. is nearly twice as heavy as a male black rhino.

v. has a hollow trunk.

5 Complete the sentences to make sentences with relative clauses. Look the animals up online if necessary.

Example: *The tiger, **which is found in Asia, is the largest of the big cats.***

1. *Spinosaurus*, _____.

2. A blue whale, _____.

3. Megalodon, _____.

Reduction of relative clauses

Some of the relative clauses we have encountered in this unit can be simplified.

The relative pronoun (*that, who, which*, etc.) can be left out if it is followed by a new subject and verb.
*The documentaries **(that) I was telling you about** deal with sea creatures.*
*The scientists **(that/who) I saw** in the documentaries were really interesting.*

If the clause is placed inside commas within a sentence, it can be changed.
*My brother, **(who is)** a filmmaker, created a documentary about manta rays.*

If the verb attached to the subject is in the passive voice, it can be left out.
*One of the documentaries is about a new species **(that/which was)** discovered last year.*

REMEMBER

When the relative pronoun (*that, who, which*) is the subject of the clause, it cannot be deleted. To reduce the clause we can use the verb in the *-ing* form.
*The biologist **who studies** manta rays lives in Mozambique.* ⟶ *The biologist **studying** manta rays lives in Mozambique.*

1 **Rewrite the sentences, reducing the clauses.**

Example: *My favourite TV programme last year, which was shot in Tsavo National Park in Kenya, followed an elephant herd.*
  My favourite TV programme last year, shot in Tsavo National Park in Kenya, followed an elephant herd.

1. The best wildlife photograph I saw last year, which was taken in the Sea of Cortez, was of a blue whale tail.

   _____

2. The Sea of Cortez, which sits between the Baja California peninsula and the Mexican mainland, is a haven for many whale species.

   _____

3. The explorer, who was stuck on the Arctic pack ice for weeks, managed to make valuable observations of polar bears.

   _____

4. My grandfather, who will be in Patagonia for several months, hopes to see a puma next year.

   _____

5. The botanist who I met in South Africa taught me a lot about the different grasses animals eat.

   _____

2 **These clauses have been reduced.** Write the full clause.

Example: *My mother, an artist ...*   ***My mother, who is an artist ...***

1. The animal I was desperate to see ...   _____

2. The species discovered only last year ... _____

3. The herd followed in the programme ... _____

4. The tree climbed by the scientists ...   _____

5. The people I met in the field ...   _____

3 **Choose the clause that can be reduced and cross out the unnecessary words.**

Example: *The programme* **which was** *shown on television was about a scientist* **who** *studies whales in Antarctica.*

1. The documentary, **which was** about giant trees, showed an ecosystem **which** depended on them.

2. The programme, **which goes** out tonight, reveals an ecosystem **which is** dependent on elephants.

3. Blue whales, **which are** found in every ocean, are the subjects of a new film **which will be** broadcast next year.

4. Whale sharks, **which are** the world's largest fish, are filter feeders **that** depend on plankton.

5. Giant trees are found across the globe, but it is the largest, **which are** found in California, **which are** the subject of my study

4 **Use the prompts and your own ideas to write sentences.** Include reduced relative clauses.

Example: *The explorer* **I admire the most is Alexander von Humboldt, for his curiosity and sense of adventure.** (**Note:** 'I admire' is a reduction of 'that/who I admire'.)

1. The reptile _____.

2. The tree _____.

3. The scientist _____.

4. The insect _____.

5. The marine mammal _____.

6. The documentary _____.

WRITING

Write three sentences about a modern giant in both reduced and full form.

Example: *The zoologist,* ***who specialises*** *in mega fauna, is concerned about threats to African species such as the elephant.*

The zoologist, ***specialising*** *in mega fauna, is concerned about threats to African species such as the elephant.*

Wish and *if only*

Adverbs

A creative way to bring the dog along, Taipei

We use *wish/if only* + past simple to express wishes for the present or the future. Remember to use *were* for the verb *be*.

If only we were at the technology fair! We could see a demonstration of the EEG headset.

We use *wish/if only* + past perfect to express regrets to do with situations which cannot be changed.

I wish my teacher had told me about the fair before today.

We also use *wish/if only* with *would* to express annoyance or criticism about the present.

I wish the invitations would go directly to students.

1 **Complete the sentences with the past simple or past perfect of the verb in brackets.**

Example: *If only we **had worked** harder on the project. (work)*

1. I wish you _____ my assistant on the project this year. (be)

2. If only they _____ so hasty in producing their robot, it would have worked better. (not be)

3. I wish I _____ more people at this technology fair. (know)

4. He wishes he _____ his friends their honest opinions of his robot. (ask)

5. Do you sometimes wish you _____ more time? (have)

6. If only you _____ me sooner; I would have helped you. (ask)

2 **Write wishes about the following situations.**

Example: *I don't know how to use my new smartphone.*
        I wish I knew how to use my new smartphone.

1. We haven't been invited to the science fair this year.

   _____

2. You didn't tell me about the experiment you took part in.

   _____

3. The technology is not open-source.

   _____

4. I haven't been included in the group working on robots.

   _____

5. The device is not working properly.

   _____

6. The software is not yet ready to launch.

   _____

3 **Write regrets about the situations.**

Example: *We were not able to stop the malware attacking the computer.*
If only we had been able to stop the malware attacking the computer.

1. The exhibition was cancelled.

   _____

2. The team didn't practise very hard.

   _____

3. My new phone doesn't have a long battery life.

   _____

4. I bought a computer without much memory.

   _____

5. I stayed up too late playing computer games.

   _____

6. I didn't try the virtual reality headset at the technology fair.

   _____

4 **Write sentences using the words in brackets.**

Example: *I haven't got enough time. (more)*
*I wish **I had more time.***

1. He is developing his invention in a tiny laboratory. (larger)

   He wishes _____.

2. The virus destroyed everybody's software. (antivirus programmes)

   If only _____.

3. I don't have the chance to use a 3D printer very often. (more often)

   If only _____.

4. She was talking during the demonstration. (pay attention)

   She wishes _____.

5. He is unsure of what to do in the experiment. (listen)

   If only _____.

6. She has an old desktop computer. (new tablet)

   She wishes _____.

Adverbs: Expressing different levels of intensity

Intensifiers are adverbs that make verbs, adjectives or other adverbs stronger or weaker.

Some adverbs increase the intensity of the phrase.
(+) very, really, extremely, absolutely, so, certainly, quite
*Inventor Kelvin Doe is **so** clever.*

Some adverbs decrease the intensity of the phrase.
(-) slightly, somewhat, barely, kind of, quite, a little
*Things changed **kind of** quickly for him.*

REMEMBER

In British English, **quite** can make a phrase stronger or weaker. It depends on the context.
*That mountain really is **quite** big. (+) The stress falls on big.*
*He's **quite** tall, but not as tall as me. (-) The stress falls on quite.*

1 ⟨Circle⟩ **the most likely option.**

Example: *Louis Pasteur is* ⟨*an extremely*⟩ / *a slightly important figure in the history of vaccination.*

1. The invention of the wheel **barely / fundamentally** changed the course of human civilisation.

2. Paige Brown's invention that helped to improve the quality of water **really / hardly** made a difference to the water in her local stream.

3. The internal combustion engine **barely / completely** changed people's lives.

4. Tim Berners-Lee invented the World Wide Web, **certainly / hardly** among the most important developments in recent decades.

5. The World Wide Web is **kind of / completely** different to the Internet.

6. Many people can **barely / really** imagine life without their smartphone.

7. The microchip has **certainly / sort of** been central to the development of computers.

8. The Raspberry Pi® computer is **absolutely / slightly** bigger than a credit card.

2 Complete the sentences with an adverb from the box.

~~absolutely~~	barely	extremely	quite	rather	really

Example: *After checking the figures several times, he was **absolutely** certain of his calculations.*

1. We were _____ confused by the results at first, but they made sense when we recalculated.

2. It was _____ cold at the Antarctic research station.

3. I'd worked _____ hard on my project so I was pleased to get a good result.

4. We had _____ enough time to carry out the experiment. It was a real rush.

5. Processing the results of the experiment went _____ slowly.

3 Complete the sentences with an intensifier and an adjective of your choice.

Example: *I think Steve Jobs worked **extremely hard** to develop his company's products.*

1. They tried _____ to beat their opponents.

2. It was _____ for him to remember his lines.

3. Some people have _____ water to drink.

4. His actions were _____.

5. The food at the restaurant was _____.

4 **Write five sentences about you.** In each sentence, use an adverb which decreases the intensity of the statement.

Example: ***I work reasonably hard, but not as hard as my brother.***

1. _____

2. _____

3. _____

4. _____

5. _____

WRITING

Write five wishes or regrets. Use adverbs to intensify or decrease the intensity of your statements.

Example: *I wish I understood calculus **really** well.*

Reported speech
Two- and three-word verbs

46

Boys looking at art from the *Streets of Afghanistan* exhibition, Afghanistan

Reported speech: Describing what others say

We use **reported speech** when we tell someone else what another person said (argued, explained, pointed out, suggested, asked, etc.) – we report back. We usually have to change the tense used in the direct speech when we report back, but this is not always the case (see the table below).

past simple/present perfect ⟶ past perfect
past perfect/*should*/*would* ⟶ stay the same
some modal verbs change: *must* ⟶ *had to*

We usually change the pronoun and adverbs of time and place.
'We will begin studying sculpture later **this year**.' ⟶ *She pointed out that **they** would begin studying sculpture later **that year**.*

'I'm going to the exhibition now.'	reporting happens immediately	He **says** he**'s going to** the exhibition now. (no change)
'I will go to the exhibition tomorrow.'	reporting happens the same day	He **said** he **will go** to the exhibition tomorrow.
'I will go to the exhibition tomorrow.'	reporting happens at a later date	He **said** he **would** go to the exhibition **the following day**.

1 **Report the quotations from artists.** Use verbs from the box.

suggest	~~say~~	tell	argue	point out	state	note

Example: *'I am happy to be alive as long as I can paint.' Frida Kahlo.*
Frida Kahlo said she was happy to be alive as long as she could paint.

1. 'If I create from the heart, nearly everything works: if from the head, almost nothing.' Marc Chagall.

   _____

2. 'Art is not what you see, but what you make others see.' Edgar Degas.

   _____

3. 'Look at life with the eyes of a child.' Henri Matisse.

   _____

4. 'I don't know anybody who needs a critic to find out what art is.' Jean-Michel Basquiat.

   _____

5. 'Art is a line around your thoughts.' Gustav Klimt.

   _____

6. 'If you could say it in words, there would be no reason to paint.' Edward Hopper.

   _____

2 **Rewrite the reported statements as direct speech.** Pay attention to the changes in the tense and the pronoun.

Example: *The tour guide suggested that the cave paintings had possibly been made to record significant moments in the lives of the tribe.*

'The cave paintings were possibly made to record significant moments in the lives of the tribe,' *suggested the guide.*

1. The museum guide explained that the Mona Lisa's smile was hard to read.

   _____

   the museum guide explained.

2. My professor said he'd seen Hokusai's *Great Wave* when it was on display in New York.

   _____

   said my professor.

3. My grandmother recalled when Christo and Jeanne-Claude had wrapped a Parisian bridge in fabric.

   _____

   my grandmother recalled.

4. The art teacher asked us how many pairs of animals we could find in Jacopo Bassano's picture.

   _____

   the art teacher asked.

5. The TV presenter suggested that Miró had drawn shapes and left it up to the viewer to decide what they represented.

   _____

   the TV presenter suggested.

6. The lecturer said that Rousseau painted the different greens of a jungle amazingly considering he had never seen a real jungle.

   _____

   said the lecturer.

7. My Spanish teacher said that his favourite painting had to be *Las Meninas* by Diego Velázquez.

   _____

   my Spanish teacher said.

8. My brother argued last week that graffiti was definitely an art form, and not simply vandalism.

   _____

   my brother argued last week.

WRITING

Find an explanation of a painting. Write a paragraph reporting the author's explanation and opinions of it.

Example: *The writer said that Picasso had been moved to paint Guernica to highlight the destruction caused by war.*

Many two- and three-word verbs need an object. A simple way to understand these verbs is to put them in two groups: separable verbs and inseparable verbs.

Separable verbs can be separated, or split, by the object of the verb. These are also known as phrasal verbs (usually a verb + adverb particle, e.g. *to throw away*).
*Artists want to **draw in** their viewers.* OR *Artists want to **draw** their viewers **in**.*
When the object of a **separable verb** is a pronoun, the verb must be separated.
*I'm working to **track** them **down**.*

Inseparable verbs cannot be separated. The object must go after the parts of the verb. Verbs followed by a preposition are inseparable, as the object cannot be moved around the sentence.
*Critics **rave about** the modern art exhibition at the museum. They say it's really impressive!*
Three-word verbs are always inseparable.
*A true artist **comes up with** unique ways to express herself.*

1 **Rewrite the sentences.** Separate the verbs.

Example: *He took down the painting because he didn't like it.*
He took the painting down because he didn't like it.

1. Vincent Van Gogh **cut off** his left ear.

   _____

2. The reporter managed to **track down** Pablo Picasso for an interview.

   _____

3. The art world gradually **worked out** the meaning of the painting.

   _____

4. My ideal job would be to **track down** lost and stolen masterpieces.

   _____

5. I was initially puzzled by the cubist picture, but it gradually **drew in** my gaze.

   _____

6. My art teacher looked very impressed when I **handed in** my project.

   _____

2 **Look at the pairs of sentences.** Tick the correct sentence.

Example: a. Visiting the top floor of the Musée d'Orsay always cheers up me! ☐

  b. Visiting the top floor of the Musée d'Orsay always cheers me up! ✔

1. a. After spending so much time in the museums, I finally got round to working on my own portrait. ☐

   b. After spending so much time in the museums, I finally got round on my own portrait to working. ☐

2. a. The critics are raving the new exhibition about. ☐

   b. The critics are raving about the new exhibition. ☐

3. a. The boys didn't get away pretending they were Banksy with. ☐

   b. The boys didn't get away with pretending they were Banksy. ☐

4. a. I ran paint out of before I could finish the background. ☐

   b. I ran out of paint before I could finish the background. ☐

5. a. We had planned to visit six galleries, but ended up spending all day in just one. ☐

   b. We had planned to visit six galleries, but ended spending up all day in just one. ☐

6. a. The men broke into the room and stole the valuable painting. ☐

   b. The men broke the room into and stole the valuable painting. ☐

3 **Write sentences using some of the two- and three-word verbs in the box.**

work out	take off	talk over	throw away	calm down	hold back
track down	cheer up	sort out	hand out	come up with	get away with
look down on	look forward to	~~talk about~~	depend on	lead to	

Example: Everyone is **talking about** the new David Hockney exhibition at Tate Britain.

1. _____

2. _____

3. _____

4. _____

5. _____

WRITING

Write a paragraph reporting on an artist you know about or a museum you have been to. Use two- and three-word verbs and different tenses of reported speech.

Example: I went to a lecture on the life of Vincent Van Gogh last week. I had been **looking forward to** it for a while. The speaker said that, although critics **rave about** him now, his paintings had not been popular in his lifetime.

Irregular verbs

Infinitive	Past simple	Past participle	Infinitive	Past simple	Past participle
be	were	been	leave	left	left
beat	beat	beaten	lend	lent	lent
become	became	become	let	let	let
begin	began	begun	lie (down)	lay	lain
bend	bent	bent	light	lit	lit
bet	bet	bet	lose	lost	lost
bite	bit	bitten	make	made	made
bleed	bled	bled	mean	meant	meant
blow	blew	blown	meet	met	met
break	broke	broken	overcome	overcame	overcome
bring	brought	brought	pay	paid	paid
build	built	built	put	put	put
burn	burnt	burnt	quit	quit	quit
buy	bought	bought	read	read	read
carry	carried	carried	ride	rode	ridden
catch	caught	caught	ring	rang	rung
choose	chose	chosen	rise	rose	risen
come	came	come	run	ran	run
cost	cost	cost	say	said	said
cut	cut	cut	see	saw	seen
deal	dealt	dealt	sell	sold	sold
dig	dug	dug	send	sent	sent
dive	dived	dived	set	set	set
do	did	done	sew	sewed	sewn
draw	drew	drawn	shake	shook	shaken
drink	drank	drunk	shine	shone	shone
drive	drove	driven	show	showed	shown
dry	dried	dried	shrink	shrank	shrunk
eat	ate	eaten	shut	shut	shut
fall	fell	fallen	sing	sang	sung
feed	fed	fed	sink	sank	sunk
feel	felt	felt	sit	sat	sat
fight	fought	fought	sleep	slept	slept
find	found	found	slide	slid	slid
flee	fled	fled	speak	spoke	spoken
fly	flew	flown	spend	spent	spent
forbid	forbade	forbidden	spin	spun	spun
forget	forgot	forgotten	stand	stood	stood
forgive	forgave	forgiven	steal	stole	stolen
freeze	froze	frozen	stick	stuck	stuck
fry	fried	fried	sting	stung	stung
get	got	got	stink	stank	stunk
give	gave	given	strike	struck	struck
go	went	gone	swear	swore	sworn
grind	ground	ground	sweep	swept	swept
grow	grew	grown	swim	swam	swum
hang	hung	hung	swing	swung	swung
have	had	had	take	took	taken
hear	heard	heard	teach	taught	taught
hide	hid	hidden	tear	tore	torn
hit	hit	hit	tell	told	told
hold	held	held	think	thought	thought
hurt	hurt	hurt	throw	threw	thrown
keep	kept	kept	understand	understood	understood
kneel	knelt	knelt	wake	woke	woken
knit	knitted	knitted	wear	wore	worn
know	knew	known	weave	wove	woven
lay	laid	laid	win	won	won
lead	led	led	write	wrote	written

NOTES

NOTES

NOTES

NOTES